I0087335

3:17 AM

The Unspoken Reality

Of

Addiction Unresolved

By

Cara Emerald

3:17 AM

The Unspoken Reality

Of Addiction Unresolved

Copyright 2020 by Cara Emerald

All rights reserved. No part of this publication may be reproduced, distributed or transmitted in any form or by any means, including photocopying, recording, or other electronic or mechanical methods, without the prior written permission of the publisher, except in the case of brief quotations embodied in critical reviews and certain other noncommercial uses permitted by copyright law.

Although the author and publisher have made every effort to ensure that the information in this book was correct at press time, the author and publisher do not assume and hereby disclaim any liability to any party for any loss, damage, or disruption caused by errors or omissions, whether such errors or omissions result from negligence, accident, or any other cause.

Adherence to all applicable laws and regulations, including international, federal, state and local governing professional licensing, business practices, advertising, and all other aspects of doing business in the US, Canada or any other jurisdiction is the sole responsibility of the reader and consumer.

Neither the author nor the publisher assumes any responsibility or liability whatsoever on behalf of the consumer or reader of this material. Any perceived slight of any individual or organization is purely unintentional.

The resources in this book are provided for informational purposes only and should not be used to replace the specialized training and professional judgment of a health care or mental health care professional.

Neither the author nor the publisher can be held responsible for the use of the information provided within this book. Please always consult a trained professional before making any decision regarding treatment of yourself or others.

ACKNOWLEDGEMENT

When I wrote 3:17 a.m., not for a moment did I think that I would be able to impact people with the words I wrote. I was merely searching for a way to get the words out in the midst of all of my suffering.

I was a social work major struggling with several mental disorders. I refused to believe that I would be of any help to anyone. When I started writing, I did not regret what had happened to me. I was grateful for my mental disorders instead of wishing that I could be anyone else. I finally believed that God could use my circumstances for something far better than I could have ever imagined. If I could not help people as a social worker, I could help people through my poetry as an author.

Throughout the writing process, I was surrounded by encouraging, loving, and supportive friends who saw success in what I had to offer. If it were not for these people in my life, 3:17 a.m. would have never become a beacon of hope to those wrestling with addiction. Thank you for the late-night conversations where I wanted to pull the plug. Thank you for never giving up on me.

Elle Sisneros

Lisa Lopez

Micah Weaver

Colin Bruggeman

Taylor Hayes

Shannon Losak

Wyatt Churchman

Chris Bell

Nicole Ma

Kaelee O'Connell

Olivia Gorrell

Brandyn Kinsey

Rebecca Perez

Annemarie Gorrell

Tayari Williams

DEDICATION

To anyone who is fighting addiction, hold on baby doll. You have every right to absorb every emotion you are feeling. You do not need to dilute any feelings to appease anyone.

I want to let you know that rehabilitation takes time. A seed does not transform into a flower overnight.

Obtaining healing follows the same guide. I do not want to tell you to take it one day at a time. There will be moments where one day will feel like too much. Instead, I want to tell you to take it one hour at a time. You can only get stronger with every hour that passes by. If one hour sounds overwhelming, then start with fifteen minutes. Once you reach past the first fifteen minutes, try to make it to the next fifteen minutes. By continuing the process, you will make it to an hour. Before you know it, the sun begins to disappear with the moon taking its place. A day's progress will be set in stone in your recovery.

You survived temptation's impulses that took place within 24 hours. If you were able to move past the voices, I am proud of you. If you relapsed at any point that day, I am still proud of you. There is no shame or guilt.

Only a new day waiting ahead, giving you another round to fight back.

PREFACE

My circumstances grew unendurable as I reached adulthood. I was sexually harassed.

Close friendships began disintegrating. Inpatient therapy nearly cost me an acceptance letter. Despite receiving that letter, my grades suffered because of my mental disorders that consumed my time and energy. I had no motive to finish the fall semester. I dropped out of college uncertain of what the next few months were going to look like. I felt disconnected, hypervigilant, and repentant.

Self-harm, alcoholism, and bulimia failed to end any enduring pain. My addictions only kept the flame alive, severing the nerves attached to my brain. However, these struggles became the foundation for my book. I strived to bring light to those who were struggling, even if it was just for a few pages. There were times where I wanted to die. There were other times that I became close.

Here is the story of what almost was the end of my life.

3:17 AM

My voice unrecognizable
My body deteriorating

Under no circumstances
Did I think that as a child
I would spend my nights as an adult
Soaked in my blood
With a bottle of gin
Asking me for another dance
Starving myself to find peace
So, food would become one less thing to worry about

I knew where I was headed
However, I did not know the permanent circumstances
That I would begin to surround myself in

What was once a new life
Has become an unplanned fate
Where did the light go?

-D.L.

CARA EMERALD

She was always the one
Who ran up and hugged me
When she recognized my face

The one who told funny stories
To fill the empty silence in my car
So, the conversation would continue on

Her laugh is a mesmerizing note
I never hear anymore
Her sorrowful eyes
Are tattoos branded into my skull
I want to see them heal
Brought back to life again

Cuts wrapped around her wrists like cuffs
Her collarbone pressed up against her skin
Her physical health slowly began vanishing
Her mind space exhibited the same results
I decided to become her rock

Doing everything in my willpower
To keep her from going back
Only to push her forward from here
I will never be the next person
To make her feel like she is a burden

-I.H.

CARA EMERALD

I told myself
If I never felt hunger again
I would finally be happy
If only I could back up my arguments

Hunger pains are nails digging into my flesh
Drawing blood, Leaving scars
Mentally and physically
If only food was avoidable

My mind and my body are two different people
Screaming at each other back and forth
The argument never ends
Eating only leads you to gaining more weight
Food is essential for your survival
These thoughts are pure caffeine
Keeping me up until the sun shows its face

I can barely stand on my own
My pants do not fit around my waist anymore
The lining of my ribcage is becoming more visible
If only my mind would let me see that

The only voices that occupy mind
Keep reassuring me
I am still not thin enough
I will never be content with who I am
I am toxic to everyone I meet

It started with a number
How did it lead to this?

-D.L.

CARA EMERALD

How would your body know?
Your body does not understand how your mind thinks
Your body can only experience emotional pain physically

It is the only way it knows how to cope
The human body is incapable of grasping self-hatred
But it can try to power through starvation
The human body is ineffective at tolerating guilt
Which is why it turns to faintness
In hopes to finally rest

Your figure does not know why it is not getting its nutrients
Your frame cannot comprehend the mentality
Behind the fear of not being able to eat
I know you cannot go through this alone
Which is why you force your own flesh and blood
To feel the pain that only your mind understands

-I.H.

3:17 AM

Beautiful company
Entwined in vile devotion
Deceiving my gut instincts
Revealing my motives
A poisoned glass
A fatal philosophy
I choose to live by
Impaired judgment
Blurred vision
Surrendering my self-control
Anything to forget every argument
Every bad decision
Every regret
It was never about having fun.

-D.L.

CARA EMERALD

Alcohol's illusion
A siren captivating your attention
With the agenda to lead you towards destruction
Guiding you there with a sweet intoxicating taste

Instead of reaching the joy that you were chasing
You pass out on the floor
With a burning rush down your throat
You wake up
Hoping to have a warm sensation in your heart
So, you could feel normal again.

Instead you are filled with grief
Regret
Worry
The same emotions
You tried to forget the night before
This comes to show
That nothing lasts forever

-I.H.

3:17 AM

I twisted the blade in my hands
Replaying today's tape
Every soundtrack is a daunting echo
Reminding me of things I wish I did not say
Food I wish I did not eat
Areas in my life that I will never excel in

It is a voice that becomes your own.
Your pitch and sound nailed to a T
I could not notice the manipulation in the melody
It was telling me what I wanted to hear
I deserved to be in pain
I deserved to hurt
I would never be enough for anyone

When those thoughts left my mind
My arms were covered in blood
Along with my thighs
My stomach
Staining the carpet resting beneath me

Leaving its mark
As a reminder
That I am the perpetrator of my ways
I am the one in the wrong
I am the one that needs to suffer
-D.L.

3:17 AM

Cuts are meant to be scars
The same way pain is only meant to be temporary
When the moon takes over the night sky
The sun always comes back the next morning
The moon never overpowers the sun
The two correlate
One following another
Never one above the other

Agony and bliss tie in together as well
With one following the other
One will never overpower the other

It may feel the opposite
In your most vulnerable moments
The joy you are searching for will come back
You will be able to cup it into your hands like sand
You will feel the aroma attach itself to your veins
The serene feeling you are desiring
Will be in your possession for good

I know you can
I have hope that you will

-I.H.

3:17 AM

I want to dance outside of my coffin
Free as a bird when it learns to fly on its own
I can only hope to get the smallest grasp of recovery
How beautiful it must be

-D.L.

CARA EMERALD

Addiction is an excruciating era
Healing is a painful process
It goes both ways
No one is going to pave the way
Only you can do that
You decide where you go from here

Recovery starts with that first step
That first push
That longing to want to get better
There was a part of you that was tired
Of the life that you were living
It is why you are here
Standing in the middle of the road
Wondering which side to stand on

Progress is progress
No matter how big or how small
If you are able to eat lunch but not dinner
That is still progress

Think about it
You went one whole day without hurting yourself
This is not going to be easy
You already know that
Recovery can be as painful as the addiction itself
However, it is more rewarding in the end
You do not have to run the race

You just have to finish it

-I.H.

CARA EMERALD

One day
I can say
That I have been sober for five years

One day
I can say
That I have overcome bulimia

One day
I can say
That I have never been happier

One day
I believe
That I will get there

-D.L.

3:17 AM

Fighting temptation's voices is half the battle
Do not give them the power to control you like a puppet
If you cave into the venomous taste
Your wings will come apart like Icarus
Thinking that you were the one in charge
When your desires leave you to drown

Do not let this stop you
From recovering from who you used to be
You will not drown
You will not sink
You will be able to run away from your old habits

Remember the steps you have taken so far?
Let them be the adrenaline that keeps you from relapsing
I am still behind you
I have not left
You will not lose me now

-I.H.

CARA EMERALD

Despite every shot taken
Every slit on my wrist
Every set back that I have had
I am going to make you proud

-D.L

3:17 AM

Do not do this for me
Without motivation
The progress that you will make
Will have no lasting effect

Let me help you
But do not let me be the reason
Why you decided to seek help

This is all you
Every breakthrough
Every milestone
All of this is because of you

Do it for you
No one else
You are doing great
Keep going

-I.H.

CARA EMERALD

Peaceful, serene bliss
I forgot what that felt like
Welcome back old friend

-D.L.

3:17 AM

The beam in her eyes was being restored
Her laugh has become the same beautiful harmony
That I missed for so long

I could hear the positivity in her voice
The way she smiled with each sentence she spoke
She was even more stunning

Every day I get to watch her recover
Like a flower beginning to open up
She was stronger
She was more confident
The way she deserves to live

-I.H.

CARA EMERALD

Have you ever been grateful for someone
That you wish you never met?
Not because they have wronged you in any way
But because they have loved you through so much
That you do not want to imagine your life without them

-D.L.

3:17 AM

Unanswered calls
Messages left on read
This was not like her
She usually responded within the hour

I asked her if she wanted to see a movie
She never got back to me
We had plans to take a walk by the river
She never showed up

I recently spoke to her
She sounded like herself over the phone
As if that is what she wanted me to believe

What could have happened?
Every guess that I have
Is something I could never wish upon anyone
I hope she is ok

-I.H.

CARA EMERALD

When something happens to you
An altered perception of life is obtained
Framing the edges of your mind
Coating the structure of your nervous system

Explicit images obstruct your field of vision
Sheer panic blocks your airway
Your senses are on high alert

It feels like the trauma is happening again
You have to reassure yourself constantly
You are safe
It is only a flashback
Only to repeat the cycle all over again

The reliving is glossed over
In hopes of not drawing attention to yourself
So that you do not worry anyone
Pretending that you are going to be ok
Making everyday life harder
Slowly going back to your old ways
Unresponsive towards achieving the next milestone

I could not make it through the day
Without a thin piece of metal between my fingers
And the scent of gin lingering in my breath
When did existing become a form of punishment?
-D.L.

3:17 AM

Breathe with me
What happened sweet girl?
What made you do this to yourself?

Examine the blade in your right hand
As well as the bottle of gin in your left
Start to rub circles around them with your thumbs
Understand the power that you hold
Brand it into your skull

You have too much in your hands
More than enough to kill
To suffocate

Look at what you are about to do
This is not what you want
You do not want that liquor to destroy you
You want it to free you
You do not want that blade to annihilate you
You want it to distract you

You do not want to feel anything
You want to feel anything else
Then what you are feeling right now

Listen to me
You are not impenetrable
Like the words cut into your stomach

CARA EMERALD

You will burn
You will die

You cannot control whether or not you will wake up
You surrender that right
When you take that first swig
That first slit
Your body takes over from there

I do not know how you can hate yourself so much
To make you think that you are deserving of such pain
To die in such a heart-wrenching way
You deserve to feel loved

Comforted and secure
You are precious
So gentle
So kind
Do not let anymore label you differently

I cannot let you do this
Get rid of the blades
Pour out the alcohol
Do not die on me baby
Let me feel your pulse when morning comes
So I know that you made it another night

-I.H.

3:17 AM

I felt his gaze on me as I started to undress
His hands on top of mine
Guiding them to my bra straps and the inside of my
underwear
I winced at the sound of each hook starting to unclasp
It felt like I was watching the last few seconds of a time
bomb, right before it went off

His hands went down my back
Like he was trying to reassure me that everything was ok
When he made it to my hips, I knew I had lost
My last layer of protection was gone

Standing in front of the mirror
Knowing this is all that he wanted from me
I felt disgusted, Betrayed

Someone who I saw as friend
Saw me nothing more than a sex puppet
He was hoping that if he pulled the right strings
I would spread my legs and give him what he asked for

I could not scream
I could not push him off of me
He was never there
His words formed an apparition to live out his impulses

-D.L.

CARA EMERALD

Tears do not give consent
Her gasps did not mean yes
You left her body violated
Her childhood erased
Only to remember
Your body pressed against hers
Leaving her motionless
Unable to speak
As the beginning of her life

-I.H.

3:17 AM

It does not matter how much I drink
How deep the blade penetrates
I still remember
His hands pinning me down on the bed
The way his fingertips would trace my curves
His husk whisper telling me
"Shhh it is ok"
Before the lower part of my body went numb
And the air started to grow thicker

I do not know if I can let you go through this one with me
You are going to see me at my worst.
You will have to deal with flashbacks
Nightmares
Panic attacks
I do not think you're ready for that
I could not do that to you
I am going to have to confront this trial alone
In order to keep you in my life

-D.L.

CARA EMERALD

When I saw the cuts on your stomach,
I was enraged
I was not mad at you
I was angry because you were hurting

You were feeling an unbearable amount of turmoil
I knew what had happened to you
I did not know that you went back to self-harm
As a way to cope

I did not want to think about you doing that to yourself
I cannot pretend anymore
How could I have let you do that to yourself?

I am sorry
For not noticing before
I am sorry that for even a second
You thought that you deserved this

I wish I could say more
But know this
I am not going anywhere
You did not lose me
You never will
You may not believe me at times
There will be moments where I will have to reassure you
That I am still here
But that is ok

3:17 AM

I am here for you
You will get through this
I am right behind you
In your worst moments
And in your best
It will get better
I hope one day
You will believe it for yourself

-I.H.

CARA EMERALD

He is not going to stick around
You are too broken to love
We both know where you are going to end up
Drinking until mind shuts off only temporary
Hurting yourself
Like you always do

He has already forgotten about the progress you have made
You are still the same slit covered psycho
That you have been since the day you guys met
It is the way he will see you forever

Progress will never get you anywhere
So who cares how much you drink
How many more cuts you add to your collection?
You will never go back to who you were
After what he did to you that night
-D.L.

3:17 AM

I never want you to think
That I have given up on you
I never will

I think that you are going to become
Even stronger than you were before
You are not a victim
You are a survivor

I will never understand
What it is like to feel your pain
Or see the world from your point of view
All I know is that I will always listen
I will always stand behind you
No matter what trials you will face

I meant what I said
When I told you
I was going to be a rock in your life
Only pushing you forward from here

You will come out on top
You are already making me proud
I know the person that you are going to become
She is going to be marvelous.

-I.H.

3:17 AM

Tell me that I have become too much
Treat me like the horrible human being that I see myself as
Push me away as much as I tried to do the same to you
Scream at me to the point
Where your lungs begin scorching the rest of your body
Please do what they crave
For once my demons will let me rest

-D.L.

CARA EMERALD

My heartbeat will never be yours
But that does not mean I will not try to keep you here

My steps forward will never be yours
But that does not mean I won't walk along beside you

I will stand behind my actions
I will never say these words to you out of breath
You are still making progress
Healing will never be free of setbacks

You are not what happened to you
But the person that you will blossom into after the war is
won
You are a fighter
Do not stop now

-I.H.

3:17 AM

Your gentle understanding
Your comforting gestures
They did not seem real
I did not want them to be real

In my intoxicated state of mind
With every ounce in my being
I wanted you to say
That you have had enough

I wanted you to leave
I have been down this road before
People will only put up with you for so long
Before they begin to start asphyxiating as well
From the decisions that you chose to make

You are not like the others, now are you?
You are different
You were willing to drag me to the surface
While I was fighting to stay under

You did not want to see me live like this
You genuinely cared about me
You were truly concerned for my well-being
I wish I could wrap my head around this
I did not deserve you
I deserved to rot away drunk
Alone

CARA EMERALD

Especially after the way I treated you

There is one thing I know for certain
When I start to sober up
And my head begins to pound
I will be glad that you did not leave
Despite how much I wanted you to

-D.L.

3:17 AM

I can understand why you wanted me to leave
You have had people in your life
Claim the same things that I have told you
This is not the first time you have heard these words
But this will be the first time someone has been able to
back them up

I am not mad at you for not believing me
I am hurt that so many people have misled you
Into thinking that you would not have to fight your demons
alone
Only for them to abandon you before the first brick
crumbles
They left you crushed beneath the rubble
Forcing you to put yourself back together

Sadly, you are never able to find all of the pieces
Making you think that you are nothing but a problem
I am here to reassure that you are not
And that you never will be ok?
-I.H.

CARA EMERALD

Some days I need to hear your voice
To be reassured that I am still safe
Some days I need you to tell me you are not going
anywhere
So I will be able to fall asleep at night
Some days I just need you
-D.L.

3:17 AM

I wish she realized how much she means to me
She worried ceaselessly that I was going to leave her
As if her pain were too much for me to handle

Little did she know that I had the same fear
I have helped people through their turmoil
And they never did the same in return

I never had to worry about that with her
Her gentleness remained authentic
Her pure intentions persisted
Something which is rare to find

-I.H.

CARA EMERALD

You help me see myself in a different way
You make me feel like I am worth something
I will admit that for once I am happy
I have not been able to say that in a while

You always celebrate the small victories with me
Making me feel like I have accomplished more
Then what is worth celebrating

Progress really is progress
I can make it out on top
I will take my life back

-D.L.

3:17 AM

I have never seen someone make so much progress
In a short amount of time
She went from telling me
"If I eat anything, I will purge it."
To eating 2 meals a day and keeping them down

She was able to give me the blades on numerous occasions
Her relapses were all that she noticed
I saw her making changes to stay on the right path
Every step forward is in the right direction

This is the progress I am talking about
It may not look like much to her
But to me she is taking big steps

The things that she will accomplish in her life
The lives that she will change of those she has never met
I cannot wait to see

-I.H.

CARA EMERALD

In moments of relapse
Swallowing pill after pill
I was becoming somebody
I did not want to be

I was broken
I was hostile
But you were still there
Telling me that you were not going anywhere
That I get to choose

What do you see that I do not?
I am not in the right mind
I am not who I used to be
Why do you still treat me the same?
Like you did when we first met?

So many questions are racing through my head
Maybe one day I will understand
Why you chose to stand by me during my darkest times

Knowing that I could relapse again the next day
Instead of running the other direction like the rest
You deserve more than a thank you
But those are the only words that will come out

In my anxious and vulnerable state
One thing I do know
Is when I relapse again

3:17 AM

Not if but when
I know that I have an army behind me
Supporting me with each step
Thank you for making recovery possible

-D.L.

CARA EMERALD

Watching your story unfold
I cannot help but look in awe
At the same time
It breaks my heart

The way you would flinch when I would try to give you a
hug
How your hands would shake when you were scared to talk
to me
You could not help it

You were made to feel that way
But look at you now
Your confidence radiates off your body
You are able to eat in front of me again
Your cuts are fading into scars

Your progress never goes unnoticed
Never think that you will ever let me down
You never could
No matter how far back you may go
Those are moments that will always make me proud

-I.H.

3:17 AM

You seem to be doing pretty well
You have a lot to be proud of
You have a great support system around you
Comforting you with every relapse
Cheering you on to get you to the next milestone

I do have one thing to ask
How have you been able to repay them?
In what ways have you changed their lives?
You have not been able to benefit them the same
You have been nothing but a burden
You drain their bodies free of peace
Not a single drop left to be consumed

They cannot do this forever
They want you safe
It is the only reason they have not left yet
If you did not have them in your life
Who knows who you would turn into?

I have an idea of who you will be
If they had the courage to free themselves
A mistake trapped inside an intoxicated mindset
A pill sunken whore
Making square one her permanent residence
You will never be more than what you have done

-D.L.

CARA EMERALD

You do not have to give a fraction
You deserve to have time to heal
You give a fraction by being my friend
It is not about what you do
I do not want you to do certain things to be my friend
Just be my friend

-I.H.

3:17 AM

When I was sober
I would feel everything at once
All of the anxiety
All of the turmoil
Escaping the pain was imminent

When I was drunk, I would feel disoriented
Out of reach from my own body
Not remembering how much I drank, not remembering
anything

When I was sober
Their voices would become louder and louder
Claiming that I was becoming toxic
I believed every word they spoke to me
After all, they were my best friends

When I was drunk
I transformed into their self-labeled persona
Laced in merciless oppression
Driving away any signs of affection
Nothing made me happier

In the midst of finding my balance
I became faced with troubling ambivalence
Either I sober up only to be susceptible to more suffering
Or I drink more twisting their lies into becoming the truth
I do not know which one is worse -D.L.

CARA EMERALD

Did I miss all the signs?
I recently met up with her
There were no fresh cuts
At least on her arms
She did not cancel our lunch plans
Which is usually the first sign
It could not have been a relapse
She was doing so well
I did not want to believe it
I hope that I am wrong
And that it's only
A misguided feeling in my stomach.

-I.H.

CARA EMERALD

I did not care how much I was hurting
If it meant that I did not have to see you hurt at all
It is my fault
I never wanted you to experience my sorrow
Which is why I decided to take both of our pains head on
But that was a huge mistake on my part.
All to make sure that you were happy
Even if I ended up crawling on my hands and knees
Which was another mistake I chose to make

-D.L.

3:17 AM

When it comes to a friend
I never look for ways
On how they can benefit me
I look for what is in their hearts
The way that they treat others
The person that you are
When no one is around
That's who I want as my friend

-I.H.

CARA EMERALD

All I can say
Is that I have not purged in 2 months
That I have gone 5 months without self-injury
That is all I really have going for me

I will never be beautiful in the eyes of anyone else
I will never be the smartest in my field of choice
Everything I do is meaningless
There are people who go their whole lives without hurting
themselves
There are people who have never been diagnosed with an
eating disorder
Who cares that I made it this far?

I will never be fully recovered
I will never be cheerful
Two months will never be enough
Five months will never get me anywhere in life
I do not make anyone proud
I never did

-D.L.

3:17 AM

It may not seem like much right now
But you have achieved a lot
Picture yourself a year from now
Five years from now
You will be telling your story to people
Who are in the same circumstances as you right now

You can be a push forward in someone else's recovery
An inspiration to many
Your hard work will pay off
Every step gets you somewhere
You will achieve happiness
You will feel at ease
Which is where I know you want to be

-I.H.

CARA EMERALD

You said you did not care about how much you were
hurting
If it meant that you did not have to see them hurt at all
right?
"Yes."
You want them to be happy even if it means you were dead
am I correct?
"Yes."
Then you know what to do

-D.L.

3:17 AM

Talk to me honey
What happened?
Where is all of this coming from?
Who made you feel like this?
Please call me back
If you do not want to talk about it
That is ok
At least tell me that you are safe

-I.H.

CARA EMERALD

You are such a great person
With a huge heart for others
I can tell that you are going to go far in life

I would like to apologize
For the mistakes that I have made
You deserve to be happy
I feel like I am in the way

I cannot go on anymore
It is only going to get worse from here
But that is on me

I have made a lot of bad choices
I am not good for you
I am sorry I couldn't keep going
I am sorry, being such a toxic friend
I am sorry for hurting you
At least I will never hurt you again

You can be happy now
Don't worry about me
It will all be over soon
Goodbye
-D.L.

3:17 AM

No baby!
Please no!
We love you
We do not want you to leave us

You do not see it
But you have impacted our lives
All of us have learned from you
From your humor
Your passions
With your story
The world needs more people like you

The love is there
Equally returned
The way it should be
The way you are worthy of having

You can heal
You have gone on before
I know you can do it again

Do not worry about having to do it alone
We will all be here
We will never leave
Please let us in
Please let us love you
-I.H.

CARA EMERALD

In the daze of my body slowly giving up on me
I relived my mistakes through the crack of my closet
A motion picture on the ceiling played
reminding me of every mistake that I made

I benefited no one
I was the example of what not to be
No matter how hard I tried
There was always going to be something wrong with me

I felt the last handful of pills kick in
I slowly shut my eyes
Letting my body fall limp
My airways closed off
My receptors shutting down

I could not do it anymore
Tomorrow is a promise that I cannot keep
This was it
This was the life that I lived

A girl who has been through too much
In the eyes of those who cared
A coward whose heart was narcissistic
In the eyes of those that did not

-D.L.

3:17 AM

3:17 a.m.
In her last words
She felt like she benefited no one
Little did I know that while I slept
I would receive a text from her saying goodbye
If only I had woken up

The end of her life
Painted a picture of a future
Where I would never hear her sing
In the passenger seat of my car
Or feel her arms hug me from behind
Where I would stay awake every night afterwards
To make sure everyone was ok

Silence makes it easy for me to ask
Would it have been selfish of me to keep her alive?
Would she have hated me if I did?
Did she remember that I still loved her?
Even if she no longer with me

I would still want her to know
Even when the last pill was swallowed

Another night came as I longed for her presence
I reread her text as I tried to fall asleep
Eventually I was able to do so

Suddenly I woke up
Feeling like I was no longer alone
As I turned to my side
The clock struck 3:17 a.m.
The same time she had sent that text

As I looked at the end of my bed
A faded glow of a silhouette counteracted the blackness
Bringing in wonder and confusion
As the facial features became more distinct,
All of the blood drained from my face
I was trying to process what was in front of me
It was her

The beam in her eyes was finally restored
She had no cuts on her wrist
Not even scars
No trace of a blade could be found on her skin
She looked captivating
She was so lovely
The way she had always been
Back to that day when we first met

I did not know what to say
Do I apologize for not waking up that night?
Do I wait and see if she speaks anything?

Before I could make a decision
She smiled as she slowly disappeared out of sight
Letting me know that she was going to be ok
That I was going to be ok

And that she did not forget about me either
She still knew that I loved her

The light never went away
Even if I never see her again
At least I know that she is safe

-I.H

THE LAST INTERNAL MOMENT

"Don't leave"

"I am here"

CONCLUSION

A bright future laid ahead for D.L. where she could have used her pain to inspire others who were living underneath similar circumstances. I.H. saw hope in her and I know that you did as well. Sadly, this is the reality for some who have battled addiction. Suicide is unsettlingly common in the course of someone's recovery. Hope is engulfed by a bottle of booze. Hands are tied by the culture of an eating disorder. Blades caress the skin by short circuiting the brain. Pain is exposed but can also be indescribable. For those who struggle with any form of addiction, there is nothing to be embarrassed or ashamed of. You are not a coward for misusing substances. You are not weak for relapsing after maintaining sobriety for a period of time. You are just a person.

Give yourself more grace than what you are used to. Often at times, the things that we would never tell another person are the first things that we would tell ourselves. If a loved one told you they were abusing prescribed medication, would you call them a coward for doing so? You would not because it is not a basic human response so why tell yourself the same thing? Do not compare your recovery to someone else's. Everyone is on a journey, but no one is walking down the same road. Every country does not bear the same seasons all together. Where summer is in one country, Autumn is in another.

For anyone who knows a loved one fighting addiction, Take the time to listen to their story. Do not be afraid to approach the subject but also accept if they choose not to talk about it. They might not feel comfortable or it may be a bad time to discuss such a heavy topic. If they want to open up, they will.

Vulnerability is not something that should be forced. Knowing someone who has an addiction is not the same as having that exact addiction. You know what it is like to know someone who struggles with that specific addiction and that is it. You do not understand what it is like to fight that same addiction that your loved one is struggling with. Do not feel pressured to have the right thing to say. In most cases when people open up about their struggles, they want someone who will listen and not try to fix their problems or determine their next step.

ABOUT THE AUTHOR

Cara Emerald currently resides in the state of Texas. She strives to let people know that darkness should be embraced because it is real. She writes for those who cannot describe the emotions that they feel. Affliction should not be hidden but brought out into the light to be examined and processed. A philosophy that Cara stands by is "If you are not uncomfortable, you are not healing". Her work is portrayed to be as raw as the reality that is being faced. She is not afraid to write what is real. Ms. Emerald is big into bands including My Chemical Romance, Bring Me the Horizon, Motionless in White, Sleeping with Sirens, etc. Other than the obvious which is writing, Cara's favorite hobbies include baking, embracing self-care, and watching horror narration channels on YouTube such as Corpse Husband, Mr. Nightmare, etc.

www.ingramcontent.com/pod-product-compliance
Lightning Source LLC
Chambersburg PA
CBHW071429040426
42445CB00012BA/1306